THE LEADER'S GUIDE TO THE UNplug the Christmas machine **WORKSHOP**

D1609634

THE LEADER'S GUIDE TO THE *UN*plug

**Jo Robinson and
Jean Coppock Staeheli**

the Christmas machine

WORKSHOP

**Help Your Group Create a Joyful,
Stress-Free Holiday**

Quill

WILLIAM MORROW
New York

Copyright © 1991 by Jo Robinson and Jean Coppock Staeheli

All rights reserved. No part of this book may be reproduced or utilized in any form or by any means, electronic or mechanical, including photocopying, recording, or by any information storage or retrieval system, without permission in writing from the Publisher. Inquiries should be addressed to Permissions Department, William Morrow and Company, Inc., 1350 Avenue of the Americas, New York, N.Y. 10019.

It is the policy of William Morrow and Company, Inc., and its imprints and affiliates, recognizing the importance of preserving what has been written, to print the books we publish on acid-free paper, and we exert our best efforts to that end.

Library of Congress Cataloging-in-Publication Data

Robinson, Jo, 1947–
    The leader's guide to the *unplug the Christmas machine* workshop: help your group create a joyful, stress-free holiday / Jo Robinson, Jean Coppock Staeheli.
    p.   cm.
    ISBN 0-688-11103-3
    1. Robinson, Jo, 1947–   . Unplug the Christmas machine: a complete guide to putting love and joy back into the season.   2. Christmas—Problems, exercises, etc.   3. Simplicity—Problems, exercises, etc.   4. Christmas—Psychological aspects—Problems, exercises, etc. 5. Self-help groups—Problems, exercises, etc.   I. Staeheli, Jean Coppock.   II. Robinson, Jo, 1947–   Unplug the Christmas machine.   III. Title.
GT4985.R62   1991
394.2′68282—dc20   91-12094
                                         CIP

Printed in the United States of America

2 3 4 5 6 7 8 9 10

BOOK DESIGN BY BINNS & LUBIN / BETTY BINNS

Contents

OTHER BOOKS CO-AUTHORED BY JO ROBINSON:
Full House (Little, Brown & Co., 1986)
Getting the Love You Want (Henry Holt, 1989)
The Emotional Incest Syndrome (Bantam, 1990)

A letter to the leader

Dear Workshop Leader,

This fall, you will be one of more than a thousand people sponsoring this workshop. In churches, community colleges, public schools, hospitals, and parent support groups in hundreds of cities, people like you will be helping others learn how to Unplug the Christmas Machine and create a more joyful, meaningful celebration.

As you will see by reading the *Leader's Guide*, this task is easier to accomplish than you may have imagined. Everyone wants a celebration rich in meaning—they just haven't taken the time to pinpoint what is wrong with their current practices, and they haven't received enough guidance and encouragement to make a few simple changes.

Your role as leader is to guide the participants through a self-discovery process. You don't have to be a Christmas expert to succeed at this. Your job is to help them discover a celebration that

**THE
LEADER'S GUIDE
TO THE**
✳
UN*plug the*
*Christmas
machine*
WORKSHOP
✳

is already inside them. And we will be with you every step of the way, sharing all the insights and techniques we have gathered over ten years of conducting this workshop.

Here's to your success!

Jo Robinson and Jean Staeheli

The Christmas Pledge

✳

Believing in the true spirit of Christmas
I commit myself to

✳

Remember those people who truly
need my gifts

✳

Express my love in more direct ways than gifts

✳

Examine my holiday activities in the light
of my deepest values

✳

Be a peacemaker within my circle of
family and friends

✳

Rededicate myself to my spiritual growth

✳

Introduction

This *Leader's Guide* contains complete instructions for a workshop that helps participants create a more joyful, less stressful, and more value-centered Christmas celebration. Based on a carefully designed four-step process, the workshop enables participants to tailor a celebration that meets their individual needs.

We do not advocate a particular point of view in this workshop. Instead, the workshop is a self-discovery process that allows participants to clarify their unique beliefs and combine those beliefs into a workable plan for the coming Christmas. Because of this lack of bias, our workshop is suitable for nonreligious organizations and for all religious denominations that celebrate Christmas.

The workshop is designed to meet the diverse needs of all your participants. Some people will be coming to your workshop because they want to create a more spiritual celebration. Some will seek help coping with loneliness or depression. Some will be looking for ways to enrich a bare-bones celebration, while others will be wanting to

**THE
LEADER'S GUIDE
TO THE
***

UN*plug the
Christmas
machine*
**WORKSHOP
***

simplify one that has become too elaborate. Whatever the participants' needs, the workshop will lead them step by step to their individual solutions.

We have carefully revised this *Leader's Guide* over a ten-year period so that at each point of the workshop you have the advantage of our accumulated experience. You will find conducting the workshop an enjoyable and rewarding experience—even if you have no prior workshop experience.

Overview of the workshop

There are four main exercises to the workshop.

1 The first exercise is an inventory participants take to give them the opportunity to reflect on past celebrations. By having an accurate assessment of how they've celebrated Christmas in the past, they gain a better sense of what they like and don't like about their current practices. The inventory examines nine important aspects of the holiday: holiday preparations, family and friends, finances, traditions, spirituality, gift giving, physical and emotional health, children, and charity.

2 The second exercise is a values exercise that asks participants to rank ten common Christmas values. When participants have completed this section of the workshop, they will have a better sense of what is most important to them about the celebration.

3 The third exercise is a guided fantasy that gives participants a chance to create an ideal holiday. Trapped in a mire of habits and obligations, few people take the time to dream about how deeply satisfying the celebration can be. When participants create this vision, they will gain new insight into the positive changes they wish to make.

4 The final exercise is a simple written plan that helps the participants combine traditions and practices that have worked in the past with valuable insights gained during the workshop. By defining goals and objectives, the participants create a valuable tool to guide them toward a more loving, spiritual Christmas celebration.

Each of these exercises is followed by a group discussion, which is an essential part of the workshop. We provide a variety of topics for each discussion period.

History of the workshop

We designed this workshop in 1978 at the request of the Life Planning staff at Marylhurst College in Portland, Oregon. Over the next few years, we were asked to give the workshop to community colleges, businesses, parents' groups, social service agencies, and churches of many different denominations. In 1980 we self-published the first edition of the *Leader's Guide* so that other people could lead the workshop. Through the use of this self-published guide, the workshop has been sponsored by over a thousand organizations in over five hundred cities in the United States and Canada.

At the same time we were developing this workshop, we began a broader investigation of how Americans celebrate Christmas. Through historical research, hundreds of personal interviews, and a survey of relevant holiday literature, we gained a greater understanding of how Christmas affects family life.

In 1982 we combined all of our observations into a book entitled *Unplug the Christmas Machine, A Complete Guide to Putting Love and Joy Back into the Season*. Published by William Morrow (Morrow/Quill for the paperback version), the book is now available in a substantially revised edition. (You will want to read this book prior to conducting the workshop.)

THE
LEADER'S GUIDE
TO THE
*
UN*plug the*
Christmas
machine
WORKSHOP
*

✳

Part One

✳

PLANNING THE WORKSHOP

✳

✳

✳

General comments

Although this workshop is suited to a wide variety of people and to groups of different sizes, we have a few recommendations. First, we suggest you limit the size of your seminar to around twenty-five or thirty people. Group interaction is a crucial element of this workshop, and when there are too many people involved, there is a tendency for more assertive members to dominate. (If you are a skilled workshop leader, you can accommodate a larger group by dividing the participants into smaller discussion groups several times during the course of the workshop so that everyone has an opportunity to talk freely.)

We don't recommend that you give the workshop to fewer than eight or ten people. For small groups, an informal discussion based on the book tends to work better.

Second, if your group is typical, you will have a higher percentage of women than men. There are two reasons for this: (1) in general, more women than men sign up for family enrichment seminars such as this one, and (2) women are the key orchestrators of their family celebrations. They tend to be more deeply involved in the holiday planning and are responsible for most of the tasks. At some point in the workshop you may want to initiate a discussion on the typical roles of men and women during the holiday season. This will help explain the lopsided enrollment.

THE
LEADER'S GUIDE
TO THE
✳
UNplug the
Christmas
machine
WORKSHOP
✳

Third, if you are offering this workshop to members of your church, you will have a common basis for a spiritual exploration of the holiday, and most likely this will be a primary focus. If you are offering the workshop to the general public or to a group without common religious beliefs, however, you need to be sensitive to differing religious views. You may have people with a strong Christian background, people of other faiths, and people with no religious affiliation at all.

It is our belief that all people, no matter what their religious or philosophical orientation, are searching for ways to feel connected to ideas and feelings larger than themselves, and Christmas is a time of year when this need is keenly felt. If you have an accepting and tolerant attitude, your participants will gain new appreciation for one another's unique ways of expressing this need.

Fourth, we have had workshops comprised of people from sixteen to eighty years old. As a general trend, we have observed that younger people are usually—but not always—more eager for change. Older people, with so many years of habit and tradition behind them, tend to invest more energy in keeping things the same. You may find that they want to introduce subtle changes or change more gradually.

We don't recommend that children participate in the workshop unless they are at least fourteen or fifteen years old. This workshop is designed primarily for adults and parents will have plenty of opportunity to involve their children in meaningful discussions after the workshop. (You may wish to provide additional copies of the Participant's Manual for people to take home with them to encourage this extended discussion.)

Finally, you will probably have a combination of married and single people in your group. In many groups, married people will predominate. Find out the composition of your group as soon as possible so you can tailor your remarks to the needs of your particular group. (You might ask for a show of hands of married and single people.) This way you will not let the discussion dwell exclusively on family issues while the quite different concerns of single and childless people are ignored.

Your rights and responsibilities

Purchasing this *Leader's Guide* enables you or your organization to give the workshop as many times as you wish. You may offer the workshop free as a community service or charge a fee for participation (see page 26 for a discussion of fees). In addition, you may place bulk orders for

THE
LEADER'S GUIDE
TO THE
*
UNplug the
Christmas
machine
WORKSHOP
*

our book, *Unplug the Christmas Machine,* at a special discount rate (see page 17 of the Appendix).

Purchasing the *Leader's Guide* also gives you certain responsibilities. We ask that you advertise the workshop by its given title—"Unplug the Christmas Machine"—and that you credit the authors in all your promotional material.

This *Leader's Guide* is copyrighted, and the only pages that can be reproduced without permission are the ones of the Participant's Manual, the sample flier, the agenda, the Christmas Pledge, and the book order form.

Dealing with painful feelings

As in all workshops that explore personal and family issues, there may be a few people in your group who are having more than their share of emotional difficulties. Christmas can be an especially painful time of year for them, because they are contrasting their bleak reality with the wish for a warm and beautiful celebration. According to Dr. Calvin Frederick, former chief of Emergency Health Services of the National Institute of Mental Health, during Christmas there is a 15 percent increase in the number of people who seek professional help for depression, and the actual number of depressed people is much higher.

In our experience, the most difficult problems people face at Christmas tend to be: (1) a recent death, (2) a recent divorce, (3) general loneliness, (4) drug or alcohol abuse, and (5) marriage difficulties.

This four-hour workshop is not designed to solve serious problems such as these, so do not try to be a therapist—unless, of course, you are one. Your role as workshop leader is to help people make simple changes in their family celebrations that take these difficulties into account.

Although you don't want to be in a position of trying to resolve people's deeper problems, one thing you can do to ease their burdens is to encourage them to share their concerns with the group. For example, if the discussion is dominated by those who have an overly hectic celebration—too much to do, too many people to see, too many gifts to give, too large a family, too many choices—ask if anyone in the group has one that feels too sparse. If you, yourself, have ever been lonely at Christmas, volunteering this information may give other people permission to be more open.

**THE
LEADER'S GUIDE
TO THE**
✳
UN*plug the*
*Christmas
machine*
WORKSHOP
✳

As people begin to talk about their grief, they may cry. When this happens, acknowledge their pain. "Yes, it can be very sad to go through the holiday season the first year after a divorce. You have so many memories." You can count on the other participants to be sympathetic, and, hopefully, some will share similar experiences which will help those in pain feel less alone.

Later on in the workshop, help people cope with their unhappiness through careful planning. For example, single people can be encouraged to gather together with other single people; those mourning a recent death can create a family ceremony in memory of their loved one; recently divorced people can find solace in creating new traditions. You may also want to draw their attention to sections of *Unplug the Christmas Machine* that address their specific problems.

Keep an eye out for someone in the group who may be having an especially difficult time. The word association exercise (page 33) that begins the workshop may give you important clues. People who volunteer words like "lonely," "sad," "depressed," or "isolated" are letting you know that overwork and holiday commercialism are not their main problems. Another clue is someone's lack of participation. While some participants are freely talking about their hectic lives, others may be silent because of their more serious problems. If you have a workshop participant who seems to be seriously depressed or disturbed, you may want to talk with him or her during a break or after the workshop and recommend professional counseling.

Problem solving

People will naturally look to you, the leader, for solutions to all their holiday problems. We recommend that you allow the workshop process itself to provide most of the answers. Once people have a chance to complete the initial exercises, they will have most of the insights they need to solve their own problems.

If people still have specific problems to resolve after the third exercise of the workshop (the fantasy exercise), you have two options: (1) refer them to the appropriate pages in our book for specific advice, or (2) do the optional brainstorming exercise on page 53. Often the group will come up with practical and original solutions. Remember, you don't have to be a Christmas expert. The workshop and the book will do that for you!

THE
LEADER'S GUIDE
TO THE
*
UN*plug the
Christmas
machine*
WORKSHOP
*

Workshop preparation

Prior to the workshop, you have three main responsibilities: (1) to acquaint yourself with this *Leader's Guide*, (2) to read (or reread) your copy of *Unplug the Christmas Machine*, and (3) to take care of some pre-workshop planning details.

Here is a list of your main pre-workshop planning responsibilities:

* Determine the time and location of the workshop.
* Advertise the workshop.
* Order books (optional).
* Copy the Participant's Manual.
* Arrange for child care (optional).
* Arrange for snacks, beverages, or meals (optional).
* Take care of registrations and minor bookkeeping details.

To help you organize these activities, you may wish to use this planning sheet. (All these activities will be discussed in detail in subsequent pages.)

WORKSHOP PLANNING DETAILS

Task	Who's responsible	Suggested time	Target date	Date completed
Study this guide	_____	6–8 weeks prior	_____	_____
Determine the time and location	_____	6–8 weeks prior	_____	_____
Order books	_____	4–5 weeks prior	_____	_____
Take care of publicity	_____	4–5 weeks prior	_____	_____
Arrange for child care (optional)	_____	2–3 weeks prior	_____	_____
Arrange for refreshments (optional)	_____	1–2 weeks prior	_____	_____
Copy the Participant's Manual	_____	1 week prior	_____	_____
Read the book	_____	1 week prior	_____	_____
Assemble materials	_____	1 day prior	_____	_____
Review the book and this guide	_____	1 day prior	_____	_____
Set up the room	_____	1 day prior	_____	_____
Complete an evaluation (optional)	_____	1 week after	_____	_____

SETTING THE DATE

October and early November are ideal times to sponsor the workshop. Christmas is close enough so that people are thinking about it, but far enough away so that there is time to make some changes in its celebration. However, we have given the workshop successfully at other times of the year. When we give the workshop late in the year—in early December, for example—we counsel participants to save their major changes for the following year and to treat the coming celebration as a time to: (1) make small, personal changes, (2) gather information about what they like and don't like about the holiday, and (3) begin talking about the celebration with other family members.

When the workshop is given earlier than October, there is the risk of low attendance. Who wants to think about Christmas in March or July or September? But if you are assured of a loyal gathering, this amount of lead time will give participants a lot of time to make changes.

CHOOSING THE DAY AND TIME OF DAY

Typically, the workshop is given on a Saturday from 10:00 A.M. until 2:30 P.M. (with a break for lunch) or on a Saturday or Sunday from 1:00 P.M. to 5:00 P.M.

Before you settle on a date, check to see if your workshop would conflict with other scheduled events. You might want to check church calendars, school calendars, and lists of sporting events. Be wary of three-day weekends because many people will be out of town.

Is it possible to give the entire workshop on a weeknight? Yes—provided you are willing to shorten the process. As you know, during the week people are reluctant to attend an evening event that lasts longer than two to two and a half hours.

There are several ways to shorten the workshop. You can hand out copies of the Participant's Manual ahead of time and ask people to complete the inventory exercise before coming to the workshop. (Ask them to fill out the Exercise without help from other family members; it's important they answer the questions in terms of their own experience.) You can shorten the discussion periods during the workshop. (Keep a close eye on your watch.) And you can assign the planning exercise as homework. If you ask the participants to complete the planning exercise at home, be sure that you give clear planning instructions, and that they understand the importance of creating a written plan.

If you would like to expand the workshop and offer it as a five- or six-hour, full-day seminar, include the optional brainstorming exercise (page 53), and expand the discussion period following each exercise. You may wish to add discussion topics of special interest to your group. If you are giving the workshop to your church community, for example, you could include a discussion of your church's Christmas program and ask questions like: Which church-sponsored activities enrich your spiritual life? Which ones take a great deal of effort but have only minimal value to you? If you are giving the workshop to your school community, you could have a discussion of Christmas commercialism and its effects on children. For all groups, you could add an additional discussion period right before the final planning exercise to allow the participants time to share their favorite family traditions.

FOUR-SESSION ALTERNATIVE

Church leaders frequently ask us if they can divide the workshop into four sections and offer it on subsequent Sundays as a part of their ongoing adult education programs. This is quite possible to do. Here's how the Four-Session Alternative might work. On the first Sunday, you could ask the participants to fill in the inventory exercise (Exercise 1) and discuss their reaction to previous holidays. The second Sunday they could do the values exercise (Exercise 2) and talk about their spiritual and moral values. On the third Sunday, they could do the fantasy exercise (Exercise 3) and do some imaginative thinking about Christmas yet to come. On the final Sunday, they could put all these insights into a practical plan (Exercise 4).

Ideally, the first session would take place in mid-October and the final one in mid-November to allow plenty of time for the participants to put their plans into action. (This will also leave the remainder of November and the month of December free for Advent activities or prescheduled holiday events.) Here is a possible schedule:

Suggested four-session schedule
✳ Session 1: Inventory exercise and discussion
✳ Session 2: Values exercise and discussion
✳ Session 3: Fantasy exercise and discussion
✳ Session 4: Planning exercise and discussion

Be advised that spreading the workshop over a four-week period gives you several added complications. The main one is that you are going to have people dropping in and out of the workshop. Don't be too upset by the uneven attendance. Given the reality of people's lives, it's unavoidable. And we have learned that people gain valuable insights from the workshop even if they attend just one session.

**THE
LEADER'S GUIDE
TO THE
✳**

UN*plug the*
Christmas
machine
**WORKSHOP
✳**

Another complication is the fact that if you allow people to take their workshop materials home each week, some will forget to bring them back. One workshop leader who has given the Four-Session Alternative many times told us she solved the problem by collecting the materials at the end of each session.

If you are asked to squeeze the workshop in between the early morning and midmorning worship services, you may not get your full hour. By the time people settle down, you may be left with just forty or fifty minutes. You'll have to be prepared for this eventuality and adjust your schedule accordingly. (Because the Four-Session Alternative is so popular, you will find tips on this variation throughout this guide.)

PUBLICIZING THE WORKSHOP

If you are offering the workshop to an already assembled group of people—for example, to your women's group, church group, or parents' group—it's easy to spread the word. Simply hand out fliers or post them in a central location, print a notice in your newsletter, or make use of your phone tree.

If your workshop is open to the general public, you will have to spend more time on publicity. To make sure your event is well attended, we suggest that you mail out public service announcements and list the workshop in your local newspapers and community calendars. If you would like to generate even more interest in your seminar, you can arrange to have your local radio station conduct a phone interview with Jo Robinson or Jean Staeheli, authors of this *Leader's Guide* and *Unplug the Christmas Machine*. (To make arrangements, call us at [503] 284-4676.)

On the following page is a sample press release to use as a model.
Feel free to fill in the correct information and use it as part of your publicity efforts.

Type your press release on a standard piece of white paper in a double-spaced format. Put your name, address, phone number, and organization name on the upper left-hand corner.

Where do you send your release? Look in your phone book for the phone numbers of newspapers, television stations, and radio stations who might use your copy. Call and ask for the name of the person in charge of public service information, and address your press release to that person.

Contact: YOUR NAME
ADDRESS
PHONE NUMBER
ORGANIZATION

PUBLIC SERVICE ANNOUNCEMENT

For Immediate Release (or not later than   )

UNPLUG THE CHRISTMAS MACHINE!

On (date), the (your organization) is presenting a _____-hour workshop to help people plan a more rewarding Christmas holiday.

Based on the popular book, *Unplug the Christmas Machine* by Jo Robinson and Jean Staeheli, this workshop helps people reduce their stress and increase their enjoyment by making simple changes in the celebration. Participants will be given a chance to examine their current practices, define their values, create a fantasy Christmas, then combine all their insights into a workable plan for the coming holiday season.

To date, this innovative workshop has been sponsored by over a thousand institutions in the United States and Canada.

The workshop will be held from _____ to _____ P.M. at (your location). For more information call (your contact person) at (your phone number).

THE
LEADER'S GUIDE
TO THE
*
UNplug the
Christmas
machine
WORKSHOP
*

SHOULD YOU OFFER BOOKS AT THE WORKSHOP?

This workshop stands on its own. People will gain enough information from attending your seminar to create a workable plan for next Christmas. However, we advise that you offer individual copies of *Unplug the Christmas Machine* as a part of your workshop package.

The book serves a number of purposes. It reinforces what people learn in your workshop; it offers supplemental material that you will not have time to cover; it gives specific ideas for activities and traditions; and it gives participants an easy way to share what they have learned with family and friends.

The book is inexpensive. A single copy ordered through your bookstore costs $8.95. However, as a sponsor of this workshop, you can order the book directly from the publisher at a substantial discount. (For ordering information, see page 17 of the Appendix.) Note: You should allow four to five weeks for delivery).

How will you know how many books to order? Because you have to place your order well in advance of completing registration, you may have to do some guesswork. Ask yourself: How many people have attended similar workshops in the past? What is my goal for attendance for this workshop? If you do miscalculate and order too many books, the books can always be returned or sold to people outside the workshop.

COPYING THE PARTICIPANT'S MANUAL

In the appendix at the back of this *Leader's Guide,* you will find a copy of the Participant's Manual. You will need to make a copy for each participant. (You can wait to do this until you know approximately how many people will be attending.) When you have made the copies, staple the pages of each together, place them in a binder, or fasten them with a slide-lock cover. (You may wish to make extra copies so that participants can take an extra one home to share with their children, a spouse, their extended families, or a friend.)

SETTING THE FEE

You can offer the workshop free as a part of your adult education program, or you can charge a reasonable fee. How much should you charge? If you include a copy of *Unplug the Christmas Machine* as a part of the workshop fee, we suggest charging $15.00 to $20.00 per person. Without the book, $5.00 to $10.00 is standard. You can charge any fee you wish, of course, but be aware that a significant increase may limit participation.

Some groups have offered couples a discount to encourage greater participation of reluctant husbands. (Since a married couple can share a copy of the book, a small reduction in fees is nondiscriminatory.)

We suggest that you ask the participants to preregister and pay ahead of time. This way you will have a more accurate idea of how many people will be coming—which will help in your planning—and people will treat the commitment more seriously.

If you are offering the workshop as a community service, there are several ways to reduce costs. To save on food and refreshment costs, for example, ask participants to contribute to a potluck lunch or bring their own lunch. Publicity costs can be kept to a minimum by advertising in church, school, or company newsletters and by relying on free media publicity. By using your organization's copying machine, you can reduce or eliminate the cost of reproducing the Participant's Manual. Finally, instead of ordering individual copies of *Unplug the Christmas Machine,* you can bring a display copy and take prepaid orders at the workshop.

Here is a simple bookkeeping form to help you keep track of your income and expenses.

WORKSHOP INCOME AND EXPENSES

Expenses

Cost of the *Leader's Guide*
   (deduct the first time only) $_____

Copying costs   _____

Refreshments (optional)   _____

Child care (optional)   _____

Books (optional)   _____

Mailing (optional)   _____

Other: _____   _____

_____

Total expenses: _____

Income

Registration   _____

Other income   _____

Total income   _____

Net profit or loss $_____

**THE
LEADER'S GUIDE
TO THE
***

UNplug the
Christmas
machine
WORKSHOP
*

LAST-MINUTE DETAILS

Shortly before the workshop, refresh your memory by scanning through this *Leader's Guide*. You may find it helpful to underline key words in the directions so you can find pertinent information quickly.

Write down your projected time schedule in the space labeled "Target time" on the upper right-hand corner of each of the ten steps of the workshop. During the workshop, record the actual time that you begin each step in the space labeled "Actual time" so that you can keep yourself on track.

A few days before your seminar, check through this suggested list or a list you've made and gather up all the materials you will be needing at the workshop:

_____ your *Leader's Guide*

_____ your copy of *Unplug the Christmas Machine*

_____ the participants' manuals

_____ the participants' books

_____ name tags

_____ felt pens or chalk

_____ a chalkboard or butcher paper and easel

_____ extra pencils

_____ blank sheets of paper

_____ registration information

_____ snacks or beverages

_____ other

ARRANGING THE SETTING

When you arrive at your workshop location, take some time to arrange a comfortable, informal setting. (You may want to do this a day ahead of time.) People tend to be more open and communicative when they feel at ease. Set out the tables and chairs in a circle or semicircle instead of rigid rows. Don't distance yourself by standing behind a podium—pull out a low table and put it in front of the group, or plan to sit in one of the chairs in the circle. (If there are no tables, you will need to provide magazines or other hard surfaces for people to write on.) We recommend that you wear casual clothes rather than a suit. All of these details will contribute to a warm, relaxed environment.

As soon as you have unpacked your materials, write the day's agenda on a big sheet of paper or blackboard so that participants can refer to it throughout the day. People like to have a visual reference to the overall structure of the workshop.

Your duties during the workshop

Your principle duties during the course of the day are to

✳ Keep the workshop moving along on schedule.
✳ Explain the directions for each exercise.
✳ Select the discussion topics.
✳ Equalize the discussion.
✳ Summarize the main points at the end of discussion periods.

SETTING THE TONE

In addition to these customary responsibilities, you are also responsible for establishing the tone of the workshop. It is important that you exemplify an accepting, tolerant attitude throughout the day.

One way to do this is with a technique called "mirroring" or "empathic listening," a technique with which you may be familiar. Here's how it goes. When a participant expresses a strong thought or feeling, paraphrase that comment in your own words, without adding

STANDARD WORKSHOP AGENDA

Activity*	Page	Time (in minutes)	Your schedule
1. Opening discussion	33	15–30	_____
2. Christmas inventory	36	15–20	_____
3. Inventory discussion	40	30–60	_____
4. Values exercise	43	5–10	_____
5. Values discussion	45	20–30	_____
Short Break or Lunch Break			
6. Christmas fantasy	47	15–30	_____
7. Fantasy discussion	51	20–30	_____
8. Brainstorming exercise (optional)	53	30–45	_____
9. Planning exercise	56	30–45	_____
10. Closing discussion	61	10–15	_____

*The four major steps of the workshop process are highlighted.

**THE
LEADER'S GUIDE
TO THE**

✳

UNplug the
Christmas
machine
WORKSHOP

✳

to or taking away from the content. This "mirroring" lets the participant know that you are listening without judgment.

Here's an example:

Mary: I get so frustrated trying to get everything done at Christmas that I sometimes turn into a real witch. I hate myself for the way I treat the kids.

Leader: You have so many things on your mind at Christmas and so much to do that you get angry and frustrated and you don't like the way you treat your children. Is that what you're saying?

Mary: Yes! It's maddening to try to keep the house in order, work my job, and do Christmas too.

Notice that the leader hasn't offered advice or passed judgment. All the leader has done is let the woman know that she was heard. That alone can be therapeutic. Practice this technique throughout the day. Paraphrasing not only summarizes the proceedings, it assures your group you are paying attention.

✳

Part Two

✳

CONDUCTING THE WORKSHOP

✳

✳

✳

Opening comments and first discussion *(allow 15 to 30 minutes)*

ACTUAL TIME: _____

✳ *Where are you in the workshop?* The workshop is about to begin. Give people a friendly greeting as they come in. If they are strangers to you or to one another, hand out name tags. Ask them to write their first names only in big block letters so that everyone can read them. Do not pass out copies of the Participant's Manual until just before the inventory exercise, but if you have ordered books, you can hand out the books and let people browse through them.

If the participants know one another, there will be light conversation. If they don't, the atmosphere may be quite stilted. (If people need some loosening up, you might suggest that they share an early Christmas memory with a neighbor while the group is waiting to begin.)

OPENING COMMENTS

There are a number of ways to open the discussion. If you are giving this workshop in November or early December a good opening exercise is to introduce a word association quiz by saying, "There are only ———— (fill in the correct number) days until Christmas. What are the first three words that come into your mind as I say this?"

Give people a minute or two to write down their three words, then go around the room, having people explain their choices. (In subsequent discussions, we ask for volunteers. However, at the start of the workshop, we try to hear from everybody. Shy people often need some encouragement to speak out, and we like to get them to brave the waters as soon as possible. As you have probably observed, once people have spoken for the first time, they are much more willing to participate.)

If someone gives too long an explanation of the three words, this is a clue that you might have a long-winded participant who will need to be monitored. Keep the discussion moving and assure that person that there will be more opportunities for discussion throughout the workshop.

Here are some other ways you might begin this first discussion:

* Ask the participants to think of three words that best describe their previous Christmas celebration.
* Ask them what brings them to the workshop.
* Ask them what they hope to get out of the workshop.

Keep this initial discussion brisk and to the point. Your goal is to hear a few words from everyone.

ANALYSIS

If you opened the workshop with the three-word association quiz, the three-word summaries will probably reflect mixed emotions. Common responses are conflicting combinations such as, "terrified, hopeful, frantic," "joyful, exhausted, church," "stressed-out, anxious, family." The positive words reflect warm memories and high hopes. The negative ones attest to the difficulties inherent in the Christmas celebration. Reassure your group that mixed feelings like these are common.

This first discussion will give you, as the leader, valuable insights into the problems and values of your particular group. As you listen, you may wish to make notes about issues to pursue in coming discussions. If your group is small enough, we recommend that you sketch a seating chart as you listen to the opening discussion and write down significant remarks beside each name. For example: Joan: "Wants Christmas to be more spiritual." Tanya: "Single parent." Bill: "Recently widowed." You will find that referring to this chart from time to time will help you be more sensitive to people's individual needs. (If you have a large group, just note the general composition of the group.)

THE
LEADER'S GUIDE
TO THE
*
UNplug the
Christmas
machine
WORKSHOP
*

Exercise 1: Christmas inventory

(allow 15 to 20 minutes)

✳ *Where are you in the workshop?* Using the standard format, you are about fifteen to thirty minutes into the workshop. You will notice that the participants are feeling more comfortable with you and with one another. They have just begun to explore their feelings about the holiday —some for the first time—and have learned that other people share many of their sentiments. This is one of the most important benefits of the workshop. Many people go through the holiday season making only superficial comments like, "Christmas is too commercial," without taking the time to examine their feelings.

This first main exercise, a holiday inventory, will give the participants deeper insight into these feelings and give them objective data that will allow them to make better choices in the future.

INSTRUCTIONS FOR THE INVENTORY EXERCISE

Pass out copies of the Participant's Manual if you haven't done so already. Ask everyone to turn to "Exercise 1: A Christmas Inventory" (page 3 of the Appendix) and answer all the questions on the first 10 pages. Give the participants approximately fifteen to twenty minutes to complete the exercise.

Inform the group that this is the longest written exercise of the workshop, and that there will be a discussion of the exercise as soon as everyone is through. Those that finish ahead of time can think about what they want to talk about during this discussion period. (Your copy of the Participant's Manual is in the back of the *Leader's Guide* in the Appendix, following page 62.)

COMMENTS ON THE INVENTORY EXERCISE

Following is a brief discussion of the nine separate categories of the inventory exercise. For more information on these subjects, refer to *Unplug the Christmas Machine.*

1 Holiday preparations This first section of the inventory exercise usually surprises people. While they know full well that they are busier than usual at Christmas, they invariably underestimate the amount of work involved. Also, few people realize how many of the chores are primarily the responsibility of women. Throughout history, Christmas has been a celebration of hearth and home, and logically, women have played the key role. But today, the family celebration has become increasingly elaborate and women's lives have become more diverse. Over 50 percent of all women now have outside jobs in addition to managing the household. This means that a lot of women feel overburdened by their traditional holiday role.

Women will come to different conclusions as a result of this part of the inventory. Some will make no changes in their holiday role, but will begin to give themselves well-deserved credit for all that they do for their families. Others will see the need to simplify the celebration or find some way to redistribute the work load. Many men will spontaneously feel the need to assume a more active role in the celebration.

This first part of the inventory may also help some people see that they are putting time and energy into parts of the celebration that have little value for them. This realization will be reinforced throughout the rest of the workshop.

You might suggest to participants that you use this particular list of holiday chores as a planning sheet to allocate responsibilities in the coming year.

2 Family and friends   For most participants, spending time with family and friends is one of the most important parts of Christmas. Even if they have little money to spend and little time to devote to holiday preparations—if they are surrounded by close and loving people, they will have a good Christmas.

But for some of the participants, the family reunion is disappointing. Often the problem can be traced to long-standing family difficulties, which will not be resolved in this workshop. Perhaps the main insight people will gain from this exercise is the knowledge that few of their key relationships are simple and tension-free. Human relationships are complex and when the added strain of the Christmas season is factored in, there are few families that sail through the season without periods of tension or unhappiness. A mature acceptance of this reality can add immeasurably to people's enjoyment of the holiday.

But sometimes the family tension comes from another reason—poor planning, such as trying to see too many people in too short a time, or neglecting the needs of young children—which can be remedied. This part of the inventory and the discussion period that follows may help people see that they have more control over the logistics of the family gathering than they first realized.

In the discussion period, the participants will also have a chance to become acquainted with one another's family problems. Those who are unhappy because they have too few family members will get a

THE
LEADER'S GUIDE
TO THE
*
UN*plug the
Christmas
machine
WORKSHOP
*

THE
LEADER'S GUIDE
TO THE
*
UNplug the
Christmas
machine
WORKSHOP
*

glimpse of the pressures inherent in a large family reunion, and those who complain about too hectic a pace will gain a new appreciation for their abundance of riches. Once again, these insights into their own and other people's family gatherings can lead to a more mature acceptance of the family reunion.

3 Finances As a nation, we spend billions of dollars to wish each other a Merry Christmas. And each year advertisers spend millions of dollars trying to persuade us to spend even more. ("Nothing feels like real gold.") But for many families, the amount of money spent on Christmas strains the budget and/or results in a lavish celebration that is in conflict with their values or spiritual beliefs. This part of the inventory helps the participants see how much they are actually spending and what they are spending it on.

4 Family traditions This fourth section of the inventory gives people a closer look at their holiday traditions and helps them identify which ones give them the most satisfaction. If your group is typical, you will find that some of your participants will discover that their celebrations are cluttered up by some meaningless activities, while others will realize that theirs are too empty. This exercise gives both groups of people the insight they need to plan a more comfortable level of activity.

5 The spirit of Christmas Whether they are churchgoing or not at Christmas, people want to feel connected with ideas and experiences that are larger than themselves. But frequently the very way they celebrate Christmas works against the spiritual feelings they long for. There are several common problems. (1) People may be relying entirely on church-sponsored activities for value and meaning while their family celebrations are devoid of spirituality. (2) They may be so busy with gift giving and social activities that they don't have the time or presence of mind to nurture their spiritual lives. (3) They haven't taken the time to decide what is truly important to them about the celebration. (4) Non-Christians may be overwhelmed by the task of trying to find their own meaning in a secular, commercial celebration.

This part of the inventory will also help people identify which conditions foster spiritual expression. Ironically, many of the things they have been doing at Christmas may work against the deep feelings of spirituality they are seeking.

6 Christmas presents In many American families, gift giving has eclipsed all other Christmas traditions, taking up more time, money, and energy than all the other parts of the celebration combined. And yet, when people have a chance to stop and think about it, many decide that this obsession with gift giving robs the celebration of meaning.

Some of the people in your group will be surprised by how many names they have on their gift list, how many presents they give out of habit or obligation, and how many of their gifts cost a considerable sum of money. When they see these facts in black and white, some will want to make changes. Choosing among the four fantasies listed at the end of this page of the inventory will help them clarify what kind of change to make.

7 Physical well-being You will probably hear some amused chuckles as people fill out this part of the inventory. Most people can't imagine being relaxed and renewed by the holiday season. The unwritten law is that you should push yourself to the limit in a quest for a perfect Christmas. This exercise gives participants permission to balance their bursts of energy with activities that restore their vitality and enthusiasm and will make them more loving and receptive to the people around them.

8 Children For many adults, children are the one true note of the holiday season. When Christmas seems to them little more than an excuse to eat too much, drink too much, and spend too much money, one look at a child dancing around the Christmas tree can restore their faith in the celebration. But parents often find that Christmas commercialism makes it difficult to create a spiritual, meaningful, joyful holiday for their children. This exercise will help them pinpoint the source of their problems. Some parents will find that they don't offer their children enough meaningful holiday activities. Others will find that their pace is too hectic.

9 Charity Even though charity has been an integral part of Christmas for centuries, many people will be surprised by how few charitable activities they take part in. One reason for their lack of involvement is that commercial interests encourage them to channel their resources into giving gifts to equally affluent family and friends rather than reaching out to those in need.

Another reason could be that they are so busy orchestrating a grand production they don't have the time, money, or energy to devote to the needy. Many people who complete this inventory resolve to find more ways to extend their spirit of love and generosity beyond their inner circle of family and friends.

THE
LEADER'S GUIDE
TO THE
✳
UN*plug the
Christmas
machine*
WORKSHOP
✳

Discussion of Exercise 1 *(allow 30 to 60 minutes)*

✳ ***Where are you in the workshop?*** Using the standard format, you are about thirty to fifty minutes into the workshop. The longest written exercise is over. So far, people have not had the opportunity to share what they have learned, and they will be full of insights. Some people may have made the pleasant discovery that they like more parts of their celebration than they realized. Others may have come to the opposite conclusion. But everyone will have more objective data for discussion.

One of the functions of this discussion period is to give the participants a chance to find out which of their problems are shared by others and which are unique. It will also give them a better idea of which areas of the celebration to target for future change.

It is important to note that this is not designed to be a problem-solving portion of the workshop. People may bring up a great number of problems that will seem difficult, if not impossible, to resolve. There may be a negative, complaining tone to the discussion. Reassure your group that subsequent steps of the workshop will help them find some answers, and that it would be premature to look for answers now.

(If you are following the Four-Session Alternative format, your first day will be devoted entirely to the inventory and the inventory discussion. Participants will have to wait until the next week's session to get some insight into their problems. Reassure them that the following three sessions are designed to give them some answers.)

Whichever format you are using, there is the tendency for participants to want to share solutions with one another early on in the workshop. For example, if a woman mentions that she has a problem with her children being too preoccupied with gifts, another participant may volunteer a solution: "In our family, we do such and such." You want to postpone this kind of interchange until later on in the workshop when people have had an opportunity to sort out their values and contrast their current celebrations with their fantasy celebrations. The solutions that arise from within themselves will be more meaningful.

When people insist on volunteering solutions prematurely, we ask them to write down their ideas on a sheet of paper so they can be shared later on. It's not that their ideas aren't valuable—it's just that the workshop process needs to have an opportunity to work.

Some points to keep in mind throughout the workshop:

* Remember to equalize the discussion.
* Ask direct questions of quiet participants.
* Skillfully switch the conversation away from those who dominate.
* Be alert for someone who might have serious emotional problems.
* Keep an eye on your watch.
* Summarize important points at the end of each discussion period.

THE
LEADER'S GUIDE
TO THE
*
UNplug the
Christmas
machine
WORKSHOP

(Note: If you are following the Four-Session Alternative, you will have a lot of material to cover in your first day. You will be trying to squeeze in the introductory comments, the written inventory exercise, and a discussion period. If possible, extend this session to an hour and a half. If that is not possible, you may want to hand out the inventory exercise ahead of time and have the participants bring it to the session already filled in.

Don't be distressed if time runs out and you have an opportunity to discuss only a few sections of the inventory. Just make sure that the discussion focuses on topics of high interest. One way to do this is to ask people at the very beginning of the discussion period which topics interest them most. If a subject doesn't seem engaging, quickly move on to another one.

One workshop leader has developed her own solution to the problem of too little time for this first session. Before the workshop, she rearranges the inventory questions in order of what she believes to be topics of greatest interest. Then she has the participants complete the areas of the inventory one by one, taking time to discuss each one as it is completed. She never has time to explore all nine topics, but she is assured that the central issues will be discussed. When time runs out, she asks the participants to complete the remainder of the inventory at home before the next session.)

GROUP DISCUSSION

The inventory exercise will spontaneously generate dozens of topics of conversation. You can start things off by asking a general question such as, "What are some of the things you learned from this exercise?" Or you can select one or more topics from the following list. If a topic you suggest generates little interest, go on to another. If there is a great deal of interest in a particular topic, let this discussion continue—even if that means you won't get to other topics.

Remember that this is a problem-sharing rather than a problem-solving discussion period.

If you have a very large group (more than thirty people), you can separate the participants into smaller discussion groups and have them

THE
LEADER'S GUIDE
TO THE
*
UNplug the
Christmas
machine
WORKSHOP
*

share their reactions to the inventory. Have each group choose one person to report back a few salient points (not the whole discussion) to the larger group.

Possible topics

1 What would Christmas be like in your household if there were no gifts at all?

2 How do you feel when you read the December issues of women's magazines? What messages are those magazines sending to you?

3 Describe in one sentence last year's family reunion.

4 Think back to your childhood celebration. What roles did the adults in your family play?

5 What would Christmas be like if fathers and husbands were in charge? How would women feel watching from the sidelines? Would Christmas be the same or different?

6 What do your children learn about Christmas by watching television commercials?

7 Does Christmas make it easier or harder for you to spend enjoyable time together as a family?

8 As a single person, is it easier or harder for you during the holiday season? Why?

9 We expect to be "happy" and "merry" throughout the entire holiday season. Is this realistic? What factors work against our enjoyment of Christmas?

10 How would your children react to an "old-fashioned Christmas"? Suppose your children were to wake up and find some nuts and candy, a homemade doll or toy, and an orange or doughnut in their stockings? Would they be as pleased and excited as children were a hundred years ago? What do they expect today?

Additional topics for church groups

1 If Jesus had been an invisible guest at your house last December, what would He say about the way you celebrated His birthday?

2 Jesus' first concern was always for the poor and needy. In what ways does the commercial celebration make it difficult to share His concern during the holiday season?

3 If Jesus were joining your church, how would you like to redesign your church's Christmas celebration?

4 Is it easier for you to be in touch with your spirituality at other times of the year?

5 What does it mean to you to "celebrate Jesus' birth"?

Exercise 2: Ten Christmas values
(allow 5 to 10 minutes)

✳ ***Where are you in the workshop?*** Using a standard format, you are between one and two hours into the workshop. If your group is typical, a great deal of sharing will have taken place during the inventory discussion and the trust level will have risen considerably. But people are only beginning to find solutions to their problems. While they have had an opportunity to take an objective look at their celebrations and hear about the celebrations of others, most people will need to complete all the workshop exercises before the best solutions arise.

(If you are following the Four-Session Alternative, you are beginning your second session. You may want to ask the group if they have had any insights since the last meeting. Pass out manuals to people who are new to the group and suggest that they fill out the inventory section at home.)

DIRECTIONS FOR VALUES EXERCISE

Ask the participants to turn to the second exercise in their manuals, the values exercise, and ask them to read through the ten positive statements about Christmas. If any of the statements has no meaning to them, they should cross it out. They can also add value statements of their own that are as important to them as the ones listed. Finally, ask them to rank the remaining statements in order of importance to them. *Explain that this is not a reflection of their actual practices, but of how they want Christmas to be.* The way they celebrate may be quite different from this ranking.

Ask them to assign number "1" to their highest value, number "2" to their second highest value, and so on until they have assigned all the numbers from "1" to "10" (assuming they still have ten statements). Emphasize that each statement must be assigned a separate number.

Encourage people to be spontaneous in their responses. Assure them that there are no "right" answers. Also let them know that their choices are not going to commit them to an irrevocable course of action. This exercise is merely a tool to help them clarify their values. Remind them once again to assign number "1" to their highest value.

ANALYSIS

This simple exercise helps the participants decide which of the many competing holiday activities are most important to them. Most people

Leader's notes

go through the season making hundreds of small decisions—"What should I get for Aunt Barbara?" "What kind of dressing should we put in the turkey?"—but never stop to ask themselves the larger question, "What am I celebrating?" And because they don't have this vital piece of information, they rely on habit, other people's priorities, convenience, or commercial pressures to determine the nature of their celebrations.

This is an important exercise. When we lecture, this is often the one exercise that we ask the audience to do.

Discussion of Exercise 2 (allow 20 to 30 minutes)

TARGET TIME: _____

ACTUAL TIME: _____

✳ *Where are you in the workshop?* The values exercise has given the participants an opportunity to compare their values with their practices. Most people will have discovered some discrepancies. For example, many will have realized that gift giving takes up most of their time, money, and energy, but is not as important to them as more spiritual matters.

About this time, you may notice a shift in the tone of the workshop. Now people will be spending more time talking about how they want Christmas to be, rather than how disappointing it is.

(Note: If you are following the Four-Session Alternative, you will have a shorter day today. The values exercise can be completed in a few minutes, and the values discussion is rarely as long as the discussion following the inventory exercise. If you need to lengthen the session, you could begin by talking about some of the inventory questions you couldn't cover during the previous week. Or you could initiate a longer discussion of what kinds of conditions foster spiritual growth and brainstorm on ways to provide for them during the holiday season. Another alternative is to talk about ways to spread the ten values over the entire year so that Christmas is less hectic.)

POSSIBLE DISCUSSION TOPICS

People make three common mistakes at Christmas: (1) They don't take the time to identify their values. (2) They don't practice what they believe in. (3) They don't choose between competing values. This last problem—the reluctance to choose between competing, pos-

**THE
LEADER'S GUIDE
TO THE**
✳
UN*plug the
Christmas
machine*
WORKSHOP
✳

itive values—is likely to be the main problem for many of your participants. It's not uncommon for people to want to put a "1" beside half of the value statements. In a society that is often shallow and superficial, we have few opportunities other than Christmas to express our higher values.

But when people don't choose between competing values during the holiday season, they try to do too much and everything is diminished by their frantic activity. When a spiritual celebration is of primary importance to them, and they are also making gifts, decorating their houses, giving parties, traveling to see relatives, helping out with the school music program, and volunteering at church—all worthwhile and valuable activities—they do not have the peace of mind to deepen their spirituality.

You might begin this discussion by asking: "If you were to take this exercise all over again and rank the ten statements according to the way you actually apportion your time, energy, and financial resources during the holiday season, which ones would be on top?"

Or you can choose from the following topics:

✳ Being charitable at Christmas is important to many people. Why, then, does it seem so difficult to find the time, money, or energy to reach out to those in need during the holiday season?

✳ Why do you think we try to cram so many valuable activities into one celebration?

✳ What values are reinforced by the women's magazines?

✳ Do you ever feel a conflict between wanting to spend time with your own family and being expected to spend time with your relatives?

Additional discussion topics for church groups

✳ Think back to last Christmas. How many of your spiritual activities were church-sponsored activities?

✳ How many of your family traditions have spiritual meaning to you?

✳ What would be the reaction of your family and friends if you were to eliminate gift giving and donate that money to charity?

✳ Have there been times when gift giving has felt like an extension of your spirituality? When? Have there been times when gift giving has been in conflict with your values?

Remember, it is important that you have an accepting, tolerant attitude throughout this discussion. There are no "right" or "wrong" values. This has been brought home to us time and time again in the many opportunities we have had to conduct this workshop. During one workshop that we gave to a group of about fifty people, we read through the list of the ten values and asked people to raise their hands when we read the one that was most important to them. Predictably, there was a big show of hands for the second value (spending time with the immediate family) and the fourth value (celebrating the birth of Christ). When we got to the sixth value (gift giving), only one person raised her hand, a petite woman who appeared to be in her seventies. She told us she was a Franciscan nun, and she saw Christmas not as a time to celebrate the birth of Jesus—something she did every day of her life—but as a time to make gifts for her family and friends who were scattered around the world.

During another workshop, an active church leader told the group that her highest value at Christmas was finding time to be relaxed and renewed. "I am so busy throughout the year," she said, "that I long for those few weeks of vacation. I don't volunteer at church. I don't volunteer at school. I just stay home, enjoy my family, and rest. I love it."

There are no right and wrong answers. No "shoulds." The message of this exercise is that Christmas is rich in meaning, and it is important for people to know what it is that they value and to have an opportunity to align their practices with their values.

At the end of this discussion period, suggest that the participants take their number one value (the statement that means the most to them) and write it neatly in big letters on a sheet of paper. When they go home, they can post this sheet of paper where they can see it each day of the holiday season as a form of affirmation. Reminding themselves why they are celebrating Christmas will help them make dozens of small decisions throughout each day that will contribute to a more meaningful holiday. (You may have a calligrapher in the group who could volunteer to hand-letter some of these signs.)

(Note: In the standard format you will now either break for lunch or take a shorter break.)

Exercise 3: A Christmas fantasy
(allow 15 to 30 minutes)

TARGET TIME: _____

ACTUAL TIME: _____

✳ *Where are you in the workshop?* In the standard format, you've had approximately one and a half or two and a half hours of actual workshop time and may just be coming back from a short break or a longer lunch break. If your group has just eaten, you may notice that as the blood sugar level rises, the energy level dips. (Experienced workshop leaders may find it productive to lead one of their favorite, high-energy group activities to pick up the mood.)

By this time, everyone should be feeling comfortable with you and with other participants. From now on, the group emphasis will shift

Leader's notes

even more noticeably from what is wrong with Christmas to its rich potential.

(If you are using the Four-Session Alternative, this is the beginning of your third session. Hand out copies of the Participant's Manual to newcomers and show them which exercises to complete later at home. Ask for any new insights from people who were at earlier sessions.)

DIRECTIONS FOR THE FANTASY EXERCISE

Explain to your group that this next exercise gives them an opportunity to create a fantasy Christmas holiday. For a while they get to wipe the slate clean and start out all over again, disregarding all traditions, obligations, and past compromises. Give them permission to imagine any kind of celebration they wish. They can keep the bulk of their current traditions, or eliminate them all, as the spirit moves them.

Before you begin, help your participants to get physically comfortable. Have them close their eyes and spend a few minutes breathing deeply and slowly. You may want to turn off overhead lights—especially fluorescent ones. You can put on soft music if you wish. (If you are skilled at leading relaxation exercises, you can interject your own techniques.) If yours is a Christian group, you could lead a prayer at the beginning of this exercise to help the group imagine a truly Christian celebration.

When people are completely relaxed, ask them to imagine a perfect Christmas holiday. They have many choices. They can confine their fantasy to the twenty-fourth and twenty-fifth of December or include the whole holiday season. They can magically include their favorite friends and relatives—even people who are no longer living—and make them behave any way they wish. They can fantasize any kind of physical setting from a cabin in the mountains to a palace on the Mediterranean. This will be Christmas the way they've always wanted it to be. There is only one requirement (and you should repeat this point at the end of your explanation of the exercise): Their vision must be deeply satisfying to them and fill them with peace and joy.

Tell them that once they have settled on a particular fantasy, they should enrich it with details. Encourage them to imagine the physical setting in great detail and imagine how everyone is behaving and feeling. What kind of food is there? How was it made? Is there any music? Decorations? After people have had time to flesh out their fantasies—ten minutes is usually ample—ask them to write their Christmas dream down on the blank piece of paper provided in their workbook. (Keep an eye on the word volume. Some people jot down

one or two notes; others write novels. To keep people on track, give periodic reminders about how much time they have left.)

THE
LEADER'S GUIDE
TO THE
✳
UN*plug the
Christmas
machine*
WORKSHOP
✳

ANALYSIS

The previous two exercises have used the participants' analytical skills. This fantasy exercise stimulates their imagination and brings to mind needs and desires that are usually hidden below their level of consciousness. Once they are in tune with their subconscious needs and desires, the participants may have a quite different attitude about the holiday.

Discussion of Exercise 3 *(allow 20 to 30 minutes)*

TARGET TIME: _____

ACTUAL TIME: _____

✳ *Where are you in the workshop?* Using the standard format, you are almost three hours into the workshop. Of the four main exercises, people often find this one the most enjoyable. Some people may even be reluctant to come back to reality. Most of them will be eager to share their fantasies and will want to hear how others envision a perfect celebration. The mood may now be more contemplative.

FANTASY DISCUSSION

If you have a small group, ask volunteers to read their fantasies aloud. At first, people will enjoy hearing the idiosyncratic details of each fantasy. But after a few stories are read, they may begin to notice similarities among them.

Whether you have a small or large group, draw attention to the universality of people's fantasies. To do this, you may wish to read the list of common themes below. These are elements that we have found to be present in many people's Christmas fantasies. Ask the participants to raise their hands each time an item on this list is a part of their fantasy. (Or once they hear it, wish that it *had* been.)

Common themes
✳ A quiet and serene environment
✳ Few obligations
✳ Simple or spiritual gifts
✳ A Christmas tree or other greenery
✳ Few modern distractions (TVs, stereos, etc.)
✳ Work magically taken care of or shared by many people

51

Leader's notes

* A relaxed pace to the holiday

* Candles or a fire in the fireplace

* Singing or other music

* Simple decorations

* A feeling of love and acceptance among people

Once it becomes clear to the group that most of them share the same wishes, you might ask the obvious question: "If we all want basically the same kind of Christmas, what keeps us from celebrating this way?"

A technique that works well with a larger group is one that we call "Less and More." We ask people to compare their real-life celebrations to their fantasy ones. Then we ask them to think of one thing that there is more of in their fantasy, and one thing that there is less of in their fantasy. Then we go around the room and ask people to state these observations in as few words as possible, such as "more love, less work," "more time, less pressure," "more spirituality, less materialism." We did this once in a workshop of a hundred people, and the results were quite dramatic. People were expressing the very same wish in slightly different words.

Here are some further discussion topics:

1 Which elements of your fantasy reflect wishful thinking?

2 Which elements of your fantasy are do-able?

3 How do advertisers exploit the universal Christmas dream?

Additional topics for church groups

1 If they haven't done so already, have the members of your group share the spiritual elements of their fantasies.

2 Have members talk about the parts of their fantasies that show concern for people outside their circle of family and friends.

3 Ask the group if their fantasies automatically included some of the preconditions for spirituality mentioned in the seventh section of the inventory: time alone, time spent in a worship community, a relaxed and unhurried pace to the celebration, meditation or prayer, reading from the Bible, and being in a natural setting.

Brainstorming exercise (optional)

TARGET TIME: _____

ACTUAL TIME: _____

* *Where are you in the workshop?* During the fantasy exercise, people were contrasting the black-and-white reality of their current celebrations with the richly colored possibilities of their fantasies. But how do they get from here to there? This optional brainstorming exercise helps

Leader's notes

participants bridge the gap. Depending on the needs of your group and the amount of time you have remaining, you may want to include this brainstorming exercise.

(In the Four-Session Alternative, you are now at the beginning of your final day. You may or may not have time for a short brainstorming exercise depending upon the ease with which your group can do the final planning exercise.)

DIRECTIONS FOR THE BRAINSTORMING EXERCISE

You can brainstorm as one large group or break into smaller units, depending on the size of your group. You can think of a topic of discussion that seems especially appropriate to your group, have each group choose its own topic, or select a topic from this list:

Possible topics for brainstorming

1 What are some ways that holiday gift giving can be simplified?

2 How can families and individuals combat holiday commercialism?

3 What can this (church, community group, or school) do to make Christmas more of a celebration of love?

4 What nonmaterial gifts can we give our families this holiday season?

5 How can we reduce the holiday work load but still have a rich, enjoyable celebration?

Once each group has chosen a topic, explain these rules:

✳ Each group should select one person to be a recorder. This person should write down without any hesitation each and every idea as soon as it is suggested. This person is not a judge or a critic, but a scribe.

✳ Each group has ten minutes to think of as many solutions as possible. Quantity, not quality is the goal. Can they come up with twenty solutions? Thirty? More?

✳ People should not prejudge their own responses. Ideas that at first seem silly or irrelevant may turn out to be the most creative.

✳ People should not comment on other people's suggestions, either positively or negatively.

✳ At the end of the ten-minute "brain dump," it is time to do some sorting. Have each group cross out obvious duplications, bracket similar ideas, and underline suggestions that the group finds particularly appealing. The recorder can then report these findings back to the larger group.

ANALYSIS

This exercise is fun and lively. It is a valuable way to get people out of a narrow mind-set and see the whole range of possible solutions. So much of what we do during the holiday season is done out of habit or obligation. It also gives people a chance to share their individual solutions.

Exercise 4: Making a Christmas plan

(allow 30 to 45 minutes)

✳ *Where are you in the workshop?* At this point in the workshop, your participants have been given a chance to scrutinize their past celebrations, rank their values, come up with a delightful holiday fantasy, and in some instances, think up creative solutions to sticky problems. Now is the time for them to take out their pencils and combine all these insights into a workable plan for the coming celebration.

(If you are following the Four-Session Alternative, this exercise will take place during the final day.)

This planning exercise is based on a "goals and objectives" planning process. By now, you have a good sense of the abilities of your particular group and will know how detailed to be about the instructions. Some groups can do this exercise very easily. Others will need more hand-holding. In either case, keep checking to make sure that all directions are clearly understood and let the group know you are available for individual questions throughout the planning process.

DIRECTIONS FOR PLANNING EXERCISE

Begin the planning process with the cautionary remark that even a good plan will not create a perfect Christmas. State that perfection is rare in any life experience—especially one as complex as a family celebration when the wishes and values of so many people are involved.

You will also want to explain to the group that Christmas is an emotional, tradition-bound time of year. For this reason, the participants should introduce change gradually. It might help them to think of the coming Christmas as the first step in a five-year plan.

Also mention that sometimes a change of attitude is as helpful as a change of activities. Quite a few people have gone through this workshop without making any observable changes but report back to us that they felt much more relaxed and accepting about what they do, and that this has made all the difference.

Finally—and this is a key point—stress that this is to be a *personal plan*, one that each participant can carry out by himself or herself. When the workshop is over, the participants can go back to their households or families and go through a similar planning process to come up with a family or group plan. *But the plan they will be creating*

THE
LEADER'S GUIDE
TO THE
✳
UNplug the
Christmas
machine
WORKSHOP
✳

in this workshop is one that they can carry out without any outside help, or one that they are absolutely sure will be greeted enthusiastically by all those involved.

PLANNING STEP ONE: CHOOSING TWO OR THREE GOALS

By now, most participants should have a good sense of which parts of their celebration they wish to change. To refresh their memories, give them five or ten minutes to review their manuals. As they look over the material, they can ask themselves these questions: Which parts of my inventory revealed stress and unhappiness? Which values were most important to me? Which parts of my fantasy were both deeply fulfilling and do-able?

As they do this review, they should be looking for two or three general areas that they would like to change. For example, they may decide that they would like to scale down their gift giving, eliminate a few burdensome holiday preparations, and make their celebration more spiritual.

When they have identified some general areas, the next step is to write a statement for each one that describes how they want to feel or what they want to do that is different from their current celebration. These statements should be positive and realistic. Time and budgetary limitations should also be taken into consideration.

Here are some examples of appropriate goal statements. (You may want to write these down on the blackboard.)

Appropriate goal statements

✳ I want to spend more relaxed, enjoyable time with my young children this holiday season.

✳ I would like to spend more of my time consciously celebrating the birth of Christ.

✳ I want to scale down my holiday preparations so that I can enjoy the whole season.

✳ I want to do more active, outdoor activities this holiday season.

Here are two examples of inappropriate goals:

✳ (*Wrong*) I want my husband to be sober this Christmas.

Clearly, this is an inappropriate goal, because the participant probably has little control over her husband's drinking problem. A better goal that obliquely addresses the same issue would be:

✳ (*Better*) I want to include more holiday activities that my husband actively enjoys.

Leader's notes

By having her husband more actively involved in the celebration, there is a chance that he might not drink as much. An even better goal, moreover, would be one that focuses exclusively on the participant's own enjoyment of the holiday season.

✳ (*Best*) I would like to spend more relaxed time with my closest friends this holiday season. Here's another goal that is probably ill-advised.

✳ (*Wrong*) I would like to give no material gifts this year.

Even if this is a single person in complete control of his or her own celebration, it is probably too drastic a change. A better goal would be:

✳ (*Better*) I would like to scale down my gift giving this year.

When you are sure that everyone in your group understands what constitutes a good goal statement, allow the group fifteen minutes to write down two or three positive, realistic, general sentences that reflect how they want Christmas to be. In some groups, you may find it wise to wander around the room looking at what people are writing to make sure that the concept is fully understood.

At the end of this time period, ask for volunteers to read their statements. Check each one to make sure it is a positive, personal, realistic goal.

PLANNING STEP TWO: WRITING TWO OR THREE OBJECTIVES FOR EACH GOAL

Next, ask the participants to write down two or three sentences after each goal statement that describes in detail how that goal will be accomplished. These sentences are called "objectives." Each objective clearly states the activity that is to be done, who is to do it, and when it will be accomplished. Here is an example of a goal followed by three good objectives.

GOAL STATEMENT   I want to scale down my holiday gift giving.

✳ **Objective 1**   By November 1, I will review my gift list and call up those people who I think would welcome an opportunity to spend time together rather than exchange material gifts.

✳ **Objective 2**   I will make three sachets by November 30 to give as inexpensive gifts to my friends at work.

✳ **Objective 3**   I will call my brothers and sisters by October 1 to discuss the possibility of each of us drawing a name out of a hat instead of all of us buying or making individual gifts for everybody.

Each of these objectives is specific, tied to a specific date, and realistic. Here is an example of an incorrect objective:

✳ (*Wrong*) There will be fewer presents under the tree this year.

THE
LEADER'S GUIDE
TO THE
✳
UNplug the
Christmas
machine
WORKSHOP
✳

Leader's notes

THE
LEADER'S GUIDE
TO THE
✳
*UNplug the
Christmas
machine*
WORKSHOP
✳

You might want to read this incorrect objective to your group and have volunteers tell you what is wrong with it. They should be able to see that this sentence does not describe a specific activity, does not specify a date, and does not indicate who is going to accomplish this rather murky objective. Also, it probably affects a number of people whose cooperation is not assured.

Once a correct objective is clearly understood, give your group fifteen to twenty minutes to write down their sentences.

(Note: If you are asking your participants to complete this exercise at home, you may wish to hand out a sheet listing correct and incorrect goals and objectives that they can take home with them.)

Again, with certain groups, you will need to walk around the room and make sure that everyone is writing suitable objectives. When the time is up, once again ask for people to read their sentences and critique (kindly) each one.

Final discussion (*use up the remaining time*)

TARGET TIME: _____

ACTUAL TIME: _____

✳ *Where are you in the workshop?* The workshop is almost over. Your participants have just constructed a personal, specific, and realistic plan that integrates their values, dreams, and important traditions. They will have a well-earned sense of accomplishment. They will also have a new feeling of joyful anticipation about the coming holiday.

INSTRUCTIONS FOR THE FINAL DISCUSSION

While the members of your group now have the broad outlines of a more satisfying Christmas, they may still have some specific questions. For example, a participant may have decided that she wants to make her husband a more active participant in the celebration, but not be sure how to do that. Another may want Christmas to be more exciting, but not know what kind of traditions to include.

If you haven't done so already, now is the time to introduce your group to the resources offered in *Unplug the Christmas Machine*. If they have individual copies, ask them to turn to the Contents page so you can acquaint them with the various chapters. Let them browse through the index to see the wide variety of topics that are covered.

THE
LEADER'S GUIDE
TO THE
∗
UN*plug the*
Christmas
machine
WORKSHOP
∗

If you didn't order individual copies, let them know they can leaf through your copy (or the library copy) of the book as soon as the workshop is over. If there is sufficient interest, take orders for the book as soon as the workshop is completed.

For the final exercise of the day, ask your participants to take out pencils and paper. If you started with the three-word association exercise asking them to summarize their feelings about the coming holiday, tell them that you are going to repeat the very same exercise. Tell them, "There are now ———— days until Christmas. What are the first three words that come to mind when you think about the approaching holiday?"

Give them a minute to write down their responses, then go around the room and ask each person to read his or her words. It has been our experience that for most people, all three words will now be positive, or at the very least will reflect a mature acceptance of a difficult situation. We usually hear words like "love, family, Jesus," "excited, family, love," "optimistic, church, peaceful," "relaxed, inspired, excited." (Note: If you used another opening exercise, you can still use this one to close your workshop.)

The workshop is now over. Pack up your materials, give yourself credit for a job well done, and don't forget to wish everyone a MERRY CHRISTMAS!

✻

Appendix

✻

PARTICIPANT'S
MANUAL

✻

✻

✻

Exercise 1: A Christmas inventory

HOLIDAY PREPARATIONS

Answer the questions on each of the following three pages. Then wait for further instructions.

1 Examine the list below and cross out any holiday preparations that are not likely to be part of your Christmas celebration this year. Add any that we have overlooked.

_____ Masterminding the gift list
_____ Buying stocking stuffers
_____ Making or buying stockings
_____ Making travel plans
_____ Helping out at church
_____ Helping out at school
_____ Shopping for gifts
_____ Making gifts
_____ Buying wrapping supplies
_____ Wrapping gifts
_____ Mailing gifts
_____ Making family advent preparations
_____ Planning holiday menus for immediate family
_____ Doing special grocery shopping for immediate family
_____ Doing holiday baking for family
_____ Planning family reunions
_____ Cooking and shopping for family reunions
_____ Preparing for holiday travel
_____ Putting up inside decorations
_____ Putting up outside decorations
_____ Planning a holiday party for friends

_____ Inviting friends to the party
_____ Cooking for the party
_____ Cleaning for the party
_____ Shopping for the party
_____ Cleaning up after the party
_____ Buying or cutting down a tree
_____ Decorating the tree
_____ Helping with Christmas activities at work
_____ Making or buying decorations for the house
_____ Cleaning up after Christmas
_____ Writing thank-yous
_____ Getting kids to write thank-yous
_____ Putting away decorations
_____ Disposing of the tree
_____ Taking down outside decorations
_____ Getting ready for relatives
_____ Buying or making cards
_____ Writing notes on cards
_____ Volunteering for charity
_____ Other

2 Now, put your initials beside each activity where you do most of the work.

3 Put an "X" after those activities that have little value to you, or that you do not have time to fully enjoy.

(Go on to next page) ☀

FAMILY AND FRIENDS

1 In the space below, write down the names of family and friends with whom you are likely to spend significant time this holiday season.

_____

_____

_____

_____

_____

_____

_____

_____

_____

_____

_____

_____

_____

_____

_____

_____

_____

_____

_____

_____

_____

_____

_____

2 Put a star by the names of those people with whom you have a relatively simple, uncomplicated, loving relationship.

3 Put an "X" by those people who can make you feel uncomfortable (tense, unhappy, frustrated, angry, frightened, guilty, inferior, resentful, embarrassed, sad, worried, etc.).

4 Ideally, would you like to see (1) more, (2) fewer, or (3) about the same number of people this holiday season as you did last holiday season?

(Go on to next page)

FINANCES

In addition to the obvious expense of gift giving, there are many hidden costs to Christmas. This list will help bring them to your attention.

1 Put a check by your customary holiday expenses.

____ Buying gifts
____ Craft supplies
____ Gift-wrapping expenses
____ Mailing gifts
____ Higher phone bills
____ Extra dry cleaning
____ Paying for services such as carpet cleaning, window cleaning, or general housecleaning
____ Higher food bills
____ Travel expenses (car expenses, airplane tickets, hotels, pet boarding, etc.)
____ Loss of paid work hours
____ Extra linen, bedding, etc. for company
____ Higher entertainment costs (movies, records, etc.)
____ Decorations for the tree and house
____ Tree and other greenery
____ Candles
____ Film, flashbulbs, batteries, and film developing
____ More convenience meals during the preholiday rush
____ Christmas cards
____ Postage stamps
____ Liquor
____ Catering
____ Flowers
____ New holiday clothes
____ Holiday tipping
____ Donations to charities
____ Other

2 Estimate how much you or your family spent on all of the above expenses last year. $_____

3 Do you ordinarily stick to a holiday budget? _____

4 If you are married, is there clear communication about holiday spending between you and your spouse? _____

5 Who makes most of the holiday purchases? _____

(Go on to next page)

CHRISTMAS TRADITIONS

1 What are the traditional elements of your holiday celebration? Look through this list and cross out the ones that you do not take part in and add those that are uniquely yours. (You may wish to list specific activities in the spaces provided.)

Gift exchange
Christmas stockings
Advent rituals _____

_____

_____

_____

Holiday baking
Home entertaining
Christmas activities at church _____

_____

_____

_____

Family religious traditions _____

_____

_____

_____

Ethnic traditions _____

_____

_____

_____

Outdoor decorations
Decorating the house
Decorating a tree
Cultural events _____

_____

_____

_____

_____

_____

(Go on to next page)

Singing or playing music
Family games
Charitable activities

Other special family traditions (for example, going skiing after Christmas, visiting a nursing home, special food rituals, etc.):

_____

_____

_____

_____

_____

_____

_____

2 Underline those activities that usually give you and/or your family the most pleasure.

3 Put an "X" by the activities that you do not have time to fully enjoy or that seem to have lost their meaning for you or your family.

4 What special traditions did you do as a child that you no longer do? Star those that you wish you could add to your family celebration.

_____

_____

_____

_____

_____

_____

_____

_____

_____

_____

_____

_____

(Go on to next page)

THE SPIRIT OF CHRISTMAS

Many people find that certain circumstances foster spiritual experiences.

1 Complete the following sentence by checking all the appropriate responses and adding other comments if you wish. "I tend to feel most spiritually alive when I am _____."

_____ alone
_____ in a worship community
_____ relaxed and unhurried
_____ meditating or praying
_____ reading the Bible or other religious books
_____ outdoors in a natural setting
_____ other:

2 How often were these conditions present the last holiday season?

3 (This question is to be answered by Christians who belong to a worship community.) Of all the various holiday activities offered by my church, these are the ones that help me feel most spiritually alive:

_____
_____
_____
_____
_____
_____
_____
_____
_____
_____
_____
_____
_____
_____
_____
_____
_____
_____

(Go on to next page)

CHRISTMAS GIFTS

In the space below, list all the people with whom you normally exchange gifts. (Be sure to include people who are easy to forget, such as neighbors, children of friends, co-workers, business acquaintances, etc.)

_____

_____

_____

_____

_____

_____

_____

_____

_____

_____

_____

_____

_____

_____

_____

_____

1 Put a dollar sign by the names of people for whom you normally purchase gifts that cost more than $15.

2 Imagine yourself in each of the four imaginary situations:

a You unexpectedly receive a check in the mail for $500 to spend on Christmas gifts.

b You have the next two weeks totally free of responsibilities (including your job and the care of children) so that you can devote all your time to making Christmas gifts.

c All your friends and relatives decide to scale down their gift giving this year, happily exchanging stocking stuffers instead of more elaborate gifts.

d Gifts are reserved for young children. Adults celebrate by feasting, worshipping, partying, singing, and playing games.

Which of these four imaginary situations seems most satisfying to you? _____ Be prepared to discuss why.

(Go on to next page)

PHYSICAL WELL-BEING

1 Check all of the appropriate phrases. "Compared to other times of the year, during the period from Thanksgiving to New Year's I _____."

    _____ have less free time
    _____ get less sleep
    _____ get less exercise
    _____ consume more sugar and fats
    _____ drink more alcohol
    _____ have more tasks and responsibilities
    _____ have less time to be alone
    _____ am more worried about money
    _____ spend less relaxed time with friends
    _____ have less relaxed time with my family
    _____ have more responsiblities at work
    _____ have other stresses:

2 How does this make you feel?

3 Check the rejuvenating, coping techniques that are most effective in helping you relax and unwind.

    _____ going for walks
    _____ hot baths or showers
    _____ meditation
    _____ prayer
    _____ visiting close friends
    _____ watching TV
    _____ exercise
    _____ massage
    _____ naps
    _____ reading for pleasure
    _____ yoga or other stretching exercises
    _____ time alone with your partner
    _____ other:

4 Do you do tend to do more, less, or the same amount of the above activities during Christmas?

5 Be prepared to discuss how Christmas would change if you did more of them.

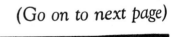

(Go on to next page)

CHILDREN

You can skip this page of the inventory if children are not an important part of your celebration.

1 Write down each of your children's (or grandchildren's) names and briefly describe each one's attitude toward Christmas.

(*Example:* Mary—Delighted by the tree, loves Christmas music, was a little frightened of Santa last year . . .

John—Preoccupied with brand-name toys, likes to make gifts for others, enjoys playing with cousins at the reunion . . .

Karen—Bored with family reunions, quite materialistic . . .)

Name	Attitude

2 List the family activities that give your children an active role in the celebration.

_____

_____

_____

_____

_____

3 List the family traditions that help your children understand the meaning of Christmas.

_____

_____

_____

(Go on to next page)

CHARITY

1 Examine the following list and cross out those charitable activities that you did *not* take part in last Christmas and add any that you participated in that we did not include.

Donations to charities
Volunteer work (list)

_____

_____

_____

_____

_____

_____

_____

Time spent with lonely people or shut-ins
Special favors for family and/or friends
Contributions to world peace
Buying holiday gifts/cards from charitable organizations
Other: _____

_____

_____

_____

_____

_____

_____

_____

_____

_____

2 Put an asterisk by those activities that are most meaningful to you.

Stop here. If you've finished ahead of others, review this inventory and think about what you would like to talk about in the discussion period that follows. What were your main areas of stress? Which parts of your celebration seem to be working well for you? Which parts of the celebration would you like to change and why?

Exercise 2: Ranking ten Christmas values

Assign the numbers "1" to "10" to each of these value statements. Place the number "1" beside your highest value, the number "2" beside your next highest value, and so on until you have assigned all the numbers. (Use each number only once.)

_____ Christmas is a time to be a peacemaker, in my family and in the world at large.

_____ Christmas is a time to spend enjoyable time with my immediate family.

_____ Christmas is a time to reunite with my relatives.

_____ Christmas is a time to celebrate the birth of Christ.

_____ Christmas is a time to create a festive, beautiful home environment.

_____ Christmas is a time to show my love and generosity through gifts.

_____ Christmas is a time to remember the poor, lonely, and needy.

_____ Christmas is a time to be active in my church community.

_____ Christmas is a time to celebrate with friends.

_____ Christmas is a time to relax and be renewed.

(Stop here and wait for further instructions)

Exercise 3: A Christmas fantasy

For this exercise, write down your vision of a deeply satisfying Christmas celebration. The only requirement is that your fantasy fill you with peace and joy.

_____

_____

_____

_____

_____

_____

_____

_____

_____

_____

_____

_____

_____

_____

_____

_____

_____

_____

_____

_____

_____

_____

_____

_____

_____

_____

_____

_____

Exercise 4: Creating a Christmas plan

My first goal for the coming celebration:

_____

_____

_____

To make this goal a reality, I am going to:

Objective 1. _____

_____

_____

Objective 2. _____

_____

_____

Objective 3. _____

_____

_____

My second goal for the coming celebration:

_____

_____

_____

To make this goal a reality, I am going to:

Objective 1. _____

_____

_____

Objective 2. _____

_____

_____

Objective 3. _____

_____

_____

(Continue on a separate sheet of paper if necessary)

15

Order Form for
The Leader's Guide to the
Unplug the Christmas Machine Workshop

The unplug the Christmas Machine workshop helps participants create more rewarding, more spiritual, and less stressful celebrations. *The Leader's Guide* contains detailed instructions for conducting the workshop as well as a copy of the Participant's Manual to be photocopied for each participant.

Please return this form to the address below with your *check or money order* for $20.00 (the cost of the book) + $3.00 (shipping and handling) + appropriate sate sales tax (or include tax exempt/resale number here _____).

Make the check payable to William Morrow and Co. Allow four weeks for delivery.

Enclosed is a check for $_____ to bill to a/c 99110.

Name: _____

Shipping address: _____

(Street address) _____

_____

Phone: (_____) _____ **Date of Order:** _____

Mail to: William Morrow and Company, Inc.
                  Special Sales
                  1350 Avenue of the Americas,
                  New York, NY 10019
                  1-800-821-1513

Please note: *Price and availability are subject to change.*

BOOK ORDER FORM

Participants in this workshop can place bulk orders of 10 or more copies of *Unplug the Christmas Machine: A Complete Guide to Putting Love and Joy Back into the Season* by Jo Robinson and Jean Coppock Staeheli. The book has a suggested retail price of $8.95. Participants qualify for the following discount rates:

1–9 copies	No discount
10–24 copies	40% discount
25–99 copies	42% discount

Please return this order form to the address below with your *check or money order* for the total cost of the books plus 10% of the total order for postage and handling. Make the check payable to William Morrow and Co., Inc. Allow four weeks for delivery.

Please include tax exempt/resale # _____ or appropriate state sales tax.

I would like to order _____ copies. Enclosed is a check for _____ to bill to a/c 99110.

NAME: _____

SHIPPING ADDRESS: _____

(Street Address) _____

_____

PHONE: (_____) _____ Date of Order: _____

MAIL TO: William Morrow and Company, Inc., Special Sales Dept., 1350 Avenue of the Americas, New York, NY 10019, 1-800-821-1513

Please note: Price and availability are subject to change.

ABOUT THE AUTHORS

Jo Robinson is a free-lance writer specializing in books about personal and social change. She is the co-author or four other books, including *Emotional Incest* and the best-selling *Getting the Love You Want.* She lives in Portland, Oregon, with her husband and son.

Jean Coppock Staeheli continues to help people make changes in their lives through her work in the Portland Health Institute's clinical programs, graduate courses and workshops, and services to health professionals. She also writes about health-related topics. Jean lives in Tigard, Oregon, with her husband and two daughters.